ANIMAL MASTERM

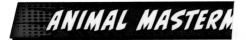

Kanzi Learns Language!

Supersmart Ape

Matata 遺

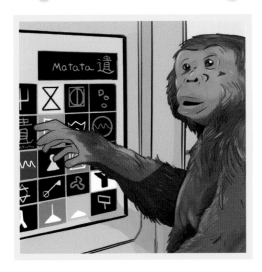

BY SARAH EASON
ILLUSTRATED BY LUDOVIC SALLÉ

BEARPORT PUBLISHING
Minneapolis, Minnesota

BEAR CLAW

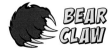

Credits: 20, © Gudkov Andrey/Shutterstock; 21, © Sergey Uryadnikov/Shutterstock; 22, © Alexwilko/Shutterstock; 22–23, © Denys Kutsevalov/Shutterstock.

Bearport Publishing Company Product Development Team
President: Jen Jenson; Director of Product Development: Spencer Brinker; Senior Editor: Allison Juda; Editor: Charly Haley; Associate Editor: Naomi Reich; Senior Designer: Colin O'Dea; Associate Designer: Elena Klinkner; Associate Designer: Kayla Eggert; Product Development Assistant: Anita Stasson

Produced by Calcium
Editor: Jennifer Sanderson; Proofreader: Harriet McGregor; Designer: Paul Myerscough; Picture Researcher: Rachel Blount

DISCLAIMER: This graphic story is a dramatization based on true events. It is intended to give the reader a sense of the narrative rather than a presentation of actual details as they occurred.

Library of Congress Cataloging-in-Publication Data

Names: Eason, Sarah, author. | Salle, Ludovic, 1985- illustrator.
Title: Kanzi learns language! : supersmart ape / by Sarah Eason ; illustrated by Ludovic Salle.
Description: Minneapolis, Minnesota : Bearport Publishing, [2023] | Series: Animal masterminds | Includes bibliographical references and index.
Identifiers: LCCN 2022035352 (print) | LCCN 2022035353 (ebook) | ISBN 9798885094306 (hardcover) | ISBN 9798885095525 (paperback) | ISBN 9798885096676 (ebook)
Subjects: LCSH: Kanzi (Bonobo)--Juvenile literature. | Kanzi (Bonobo)--Comic books, strips, etc. | Bonobo--Behavior--Juvenile literature. | Learning in animals--Juvenile literature. | Animal intelligence--Testing--Juvenile literature.
Classification: LCC QL737.P94 E27 2023 (print) | LCC QL737.P94 (ebook) | DDC 599.88515--dc23/eng/20220816
LC record available at https://lccn.loc.gov/2022035352
LC ebook record available at https://lccn.loc.gov/2022035353

Copyright © 2023 Bearport Publishing Company. All rights reserved. No part of this publication may be reproduced in whole or in part, stored in any retrieval system, or transmitted in any form or by any means, electronic, mechanical, photocopying, recording, or otherwise, without written permission from the publisher.

For more information, write to Bearport Publishing, 5357 Penn Avenue South, Minneapolis, MN 55419.

Contents

CHAPTER 1

Kanzi on Television

In 2010, a television crew interviewed Dr. Sue Savage-Rumbaugh at the Georgia State University Language **Research** Center in Atlanta.

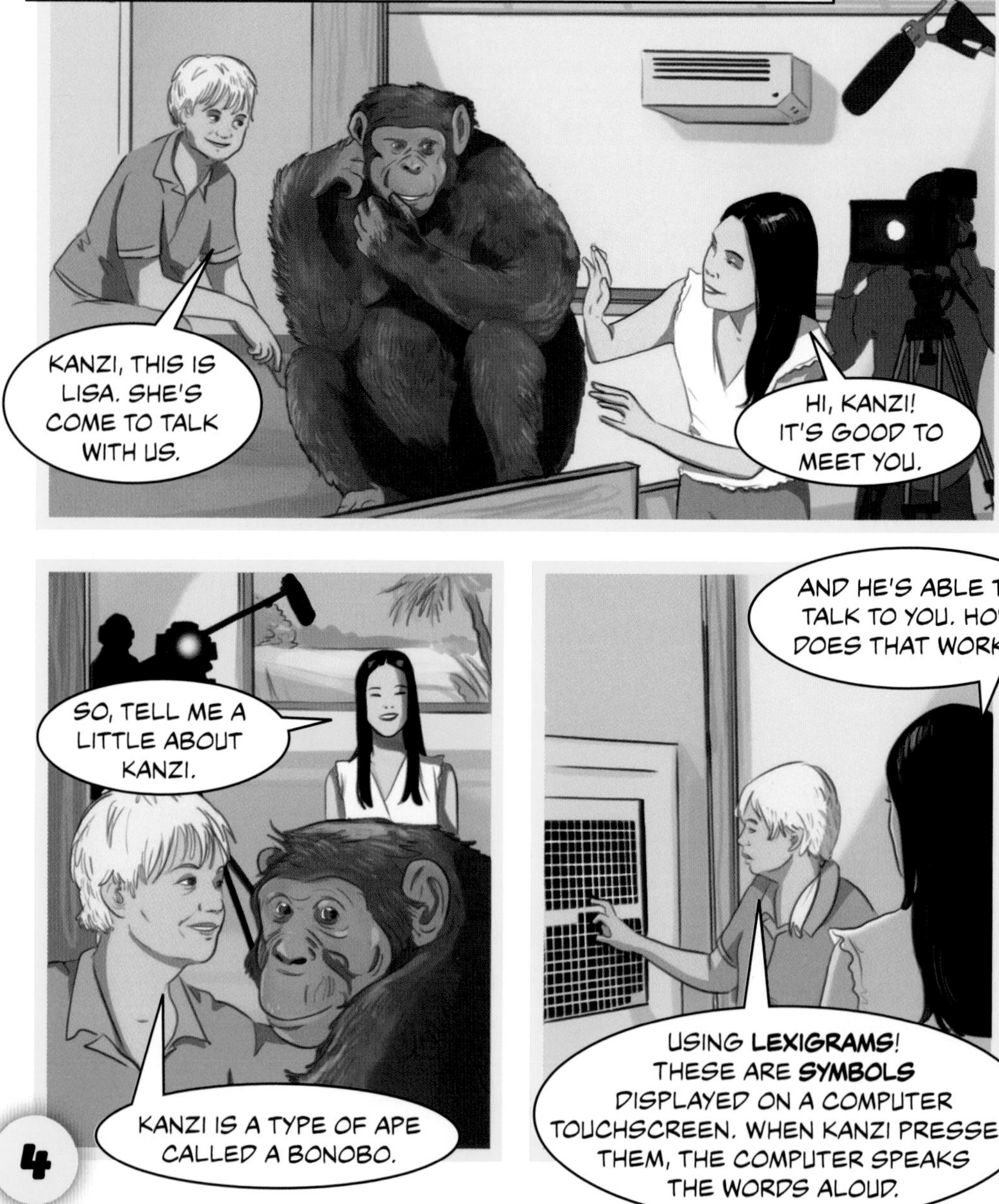
KANZI, THIS IS LISA. SHE'S COME TO TALK WITH US.
HI, KANZI! IT'S GOOD TO MEET YOU.
SO, TELL ME A LITTLE ABOUT KANZI.
KANZI IS A TYPE OF APE CALLED A BONOBO.
AND HE'S ABLE TO TALK TO YOU. HOW DOES THAT WORK?
USING **LEXIGRAMS**! THESE ARE **SYMBOLS** DISPLAYED ON A COMPUTER TOUCHSCREEN. WHEN KANZI PRESSES THEM, THE COMPUTER SPEAKS THE WORDS ALOUD.

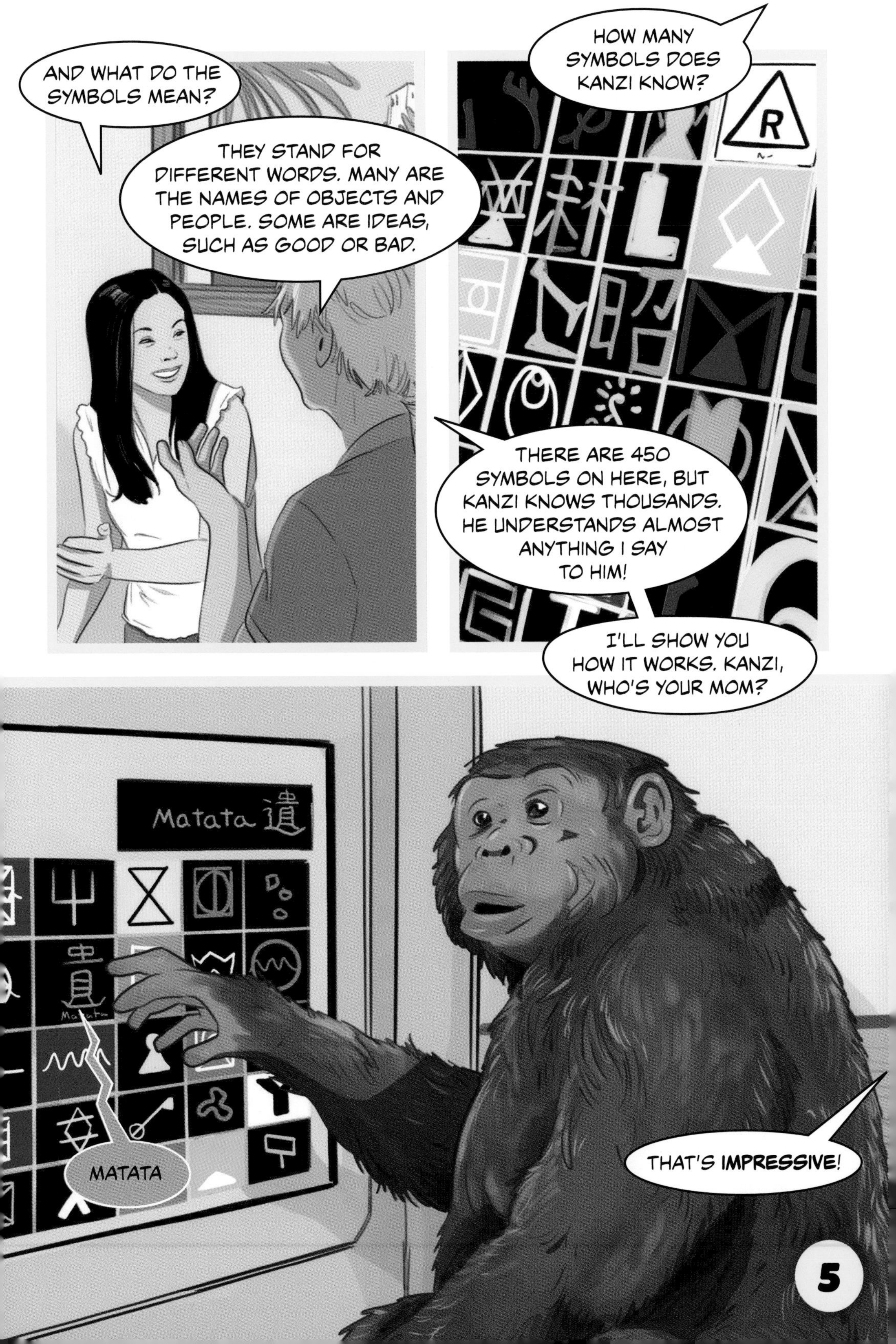
AND WHAT DO THE SYMBOLS MEAN?
THEY STAND FOR DIFFERENT WORDS. MANY ARE THE NAMES OF OBJECTS AND PEOPLE. SOME ARE IDEAS, SUCH AS GOOD OR BAD.
HOW MANY SYMBOLS DOES KANZI KNOW?
THERE ARE 450 SYMBOLS ON HERE, BUT KANZI KNOWS THOUSANDS. HE UNDERSTANDS ALMOST ANYTHING I SAY TO HIM!
I'LL SHOW YOU HOW IT WORKS. KANZI, WHO'S YOUR MOM?
Matata
MATATA
THAT'S **IMPRESSIVE**!

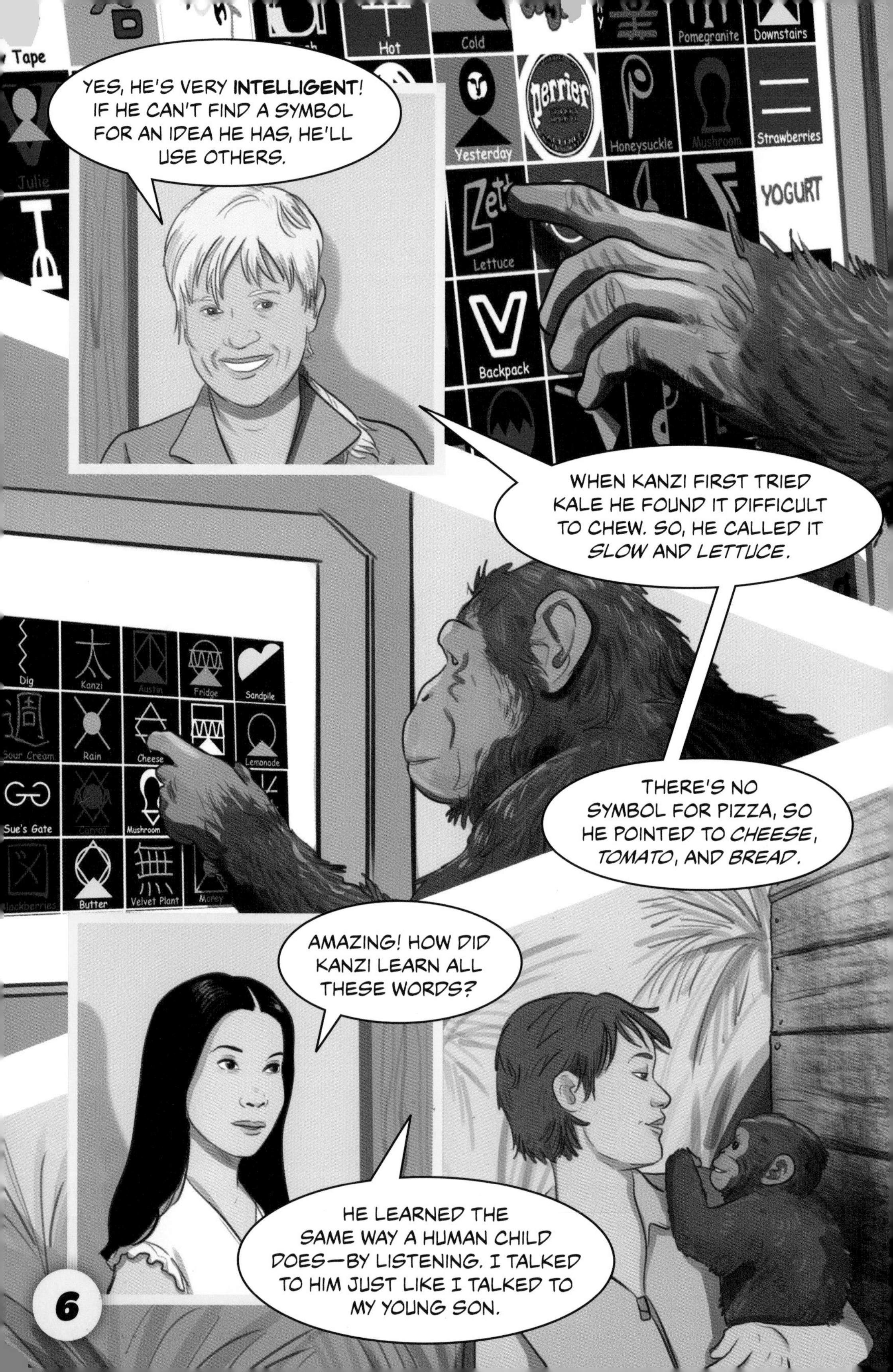
Tape
Hot
Cold
Pomegranite
Downstairs
Julie
Yesterday
Honeysuckle
Mushroom
Strawberries
YOGURT
Lettuce
Backpack
YES, HE'S VERY **INTELLIGENT**! IF HE CAN'T FIND A SYMBOL FOR AN IDEA HE HAS, HE'LL USE OTHERS.
WHEN KANZI FIRST TRIED KALE HE FOUND IT DIFFICULT TO CHEW. SO, HE CALLED IT *SLOW AND LETTUCE*.
Dig
Kanzi
Austin
Fridge
Sandpile
Sour Cream
Rain
Cheese
Lemonade
Sue's Gate
Carrot
Mushroom
Butter
Velvet Plant
Money
THERE'S NO SYMBOL FOR PIZZA, SO HE POINTED TO *CHEESE*, *TOMATO*, AND *BREAD*.
AMAZING! HOW DID KANZI LEARN ALL THESE WORDS?
HE LEARNED THE SAME WAY A HUMAN CHILD DOES—BY LISTENING. I TALKED TO HIM JUST LIKE I TALKED TO MY YOUNG SON.

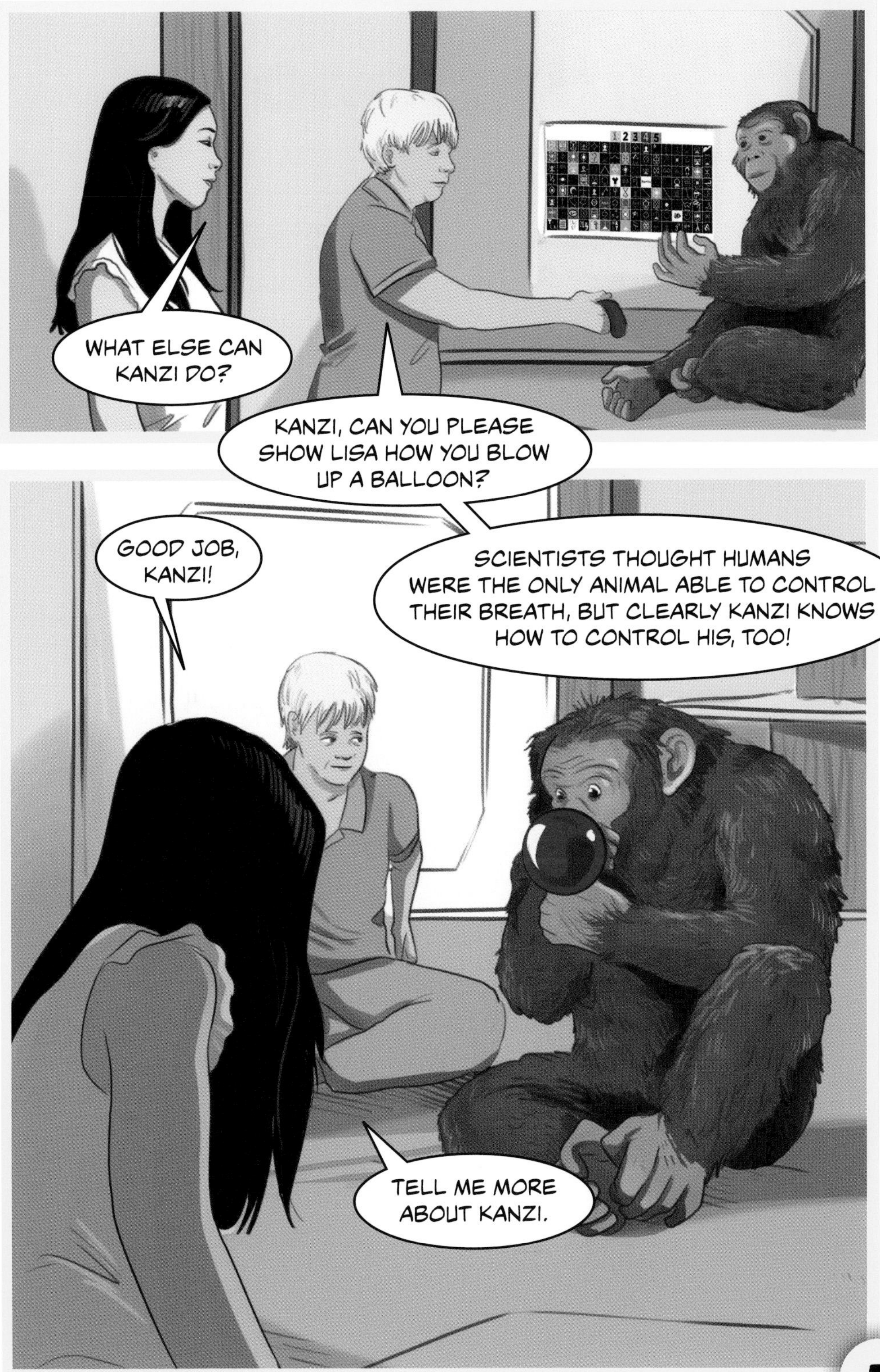
WHAT ELSE CAN KANZI DO?
KANZI, CAN YOU PLEASE SHOW LISA HOW YOU BLOW UP A BALLOON?
GOOD JOB, KANZI!
SCIENTISTS THOUGHT HUMANS WERE THE ONLY ANIMAL ABLE TO CONTROL THEIR BREATH, BUT CLEARLY KANZI KNOWS HOW TO CONTROL HIS, TOO!
TELL ME MORE ABOUT KANZI.

CHAPTER 2

Brilliant Bonobo

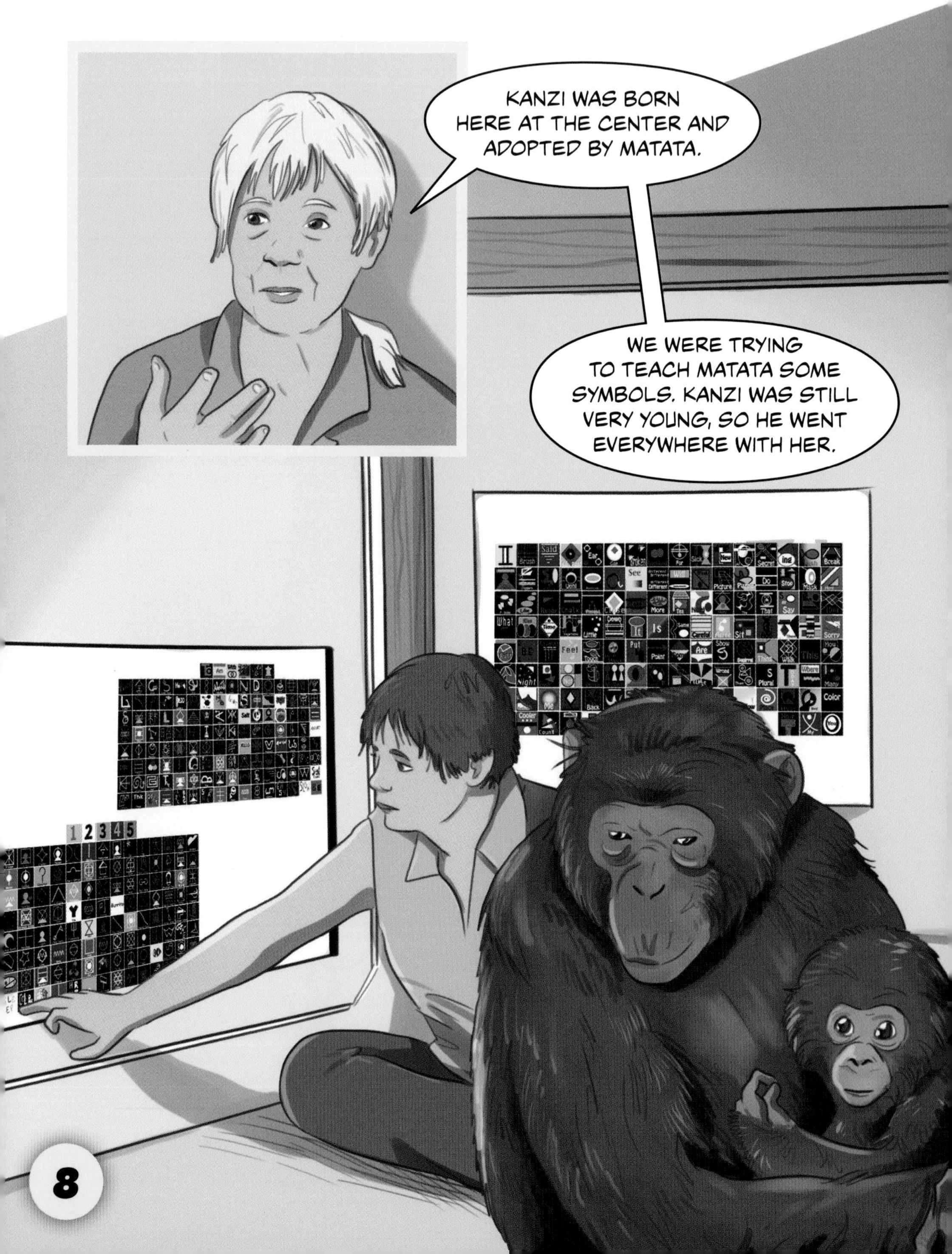

KANZI WAS BORN HERE AT THE CENTER AND ADOPTED BY MATATA.
WE WERE TRYING TO TEACH MATATA SOME SYMBOLS. KANZI WAS STILL VERY YOUNG, SO HE WENT EVERYWHERE WITH HER.

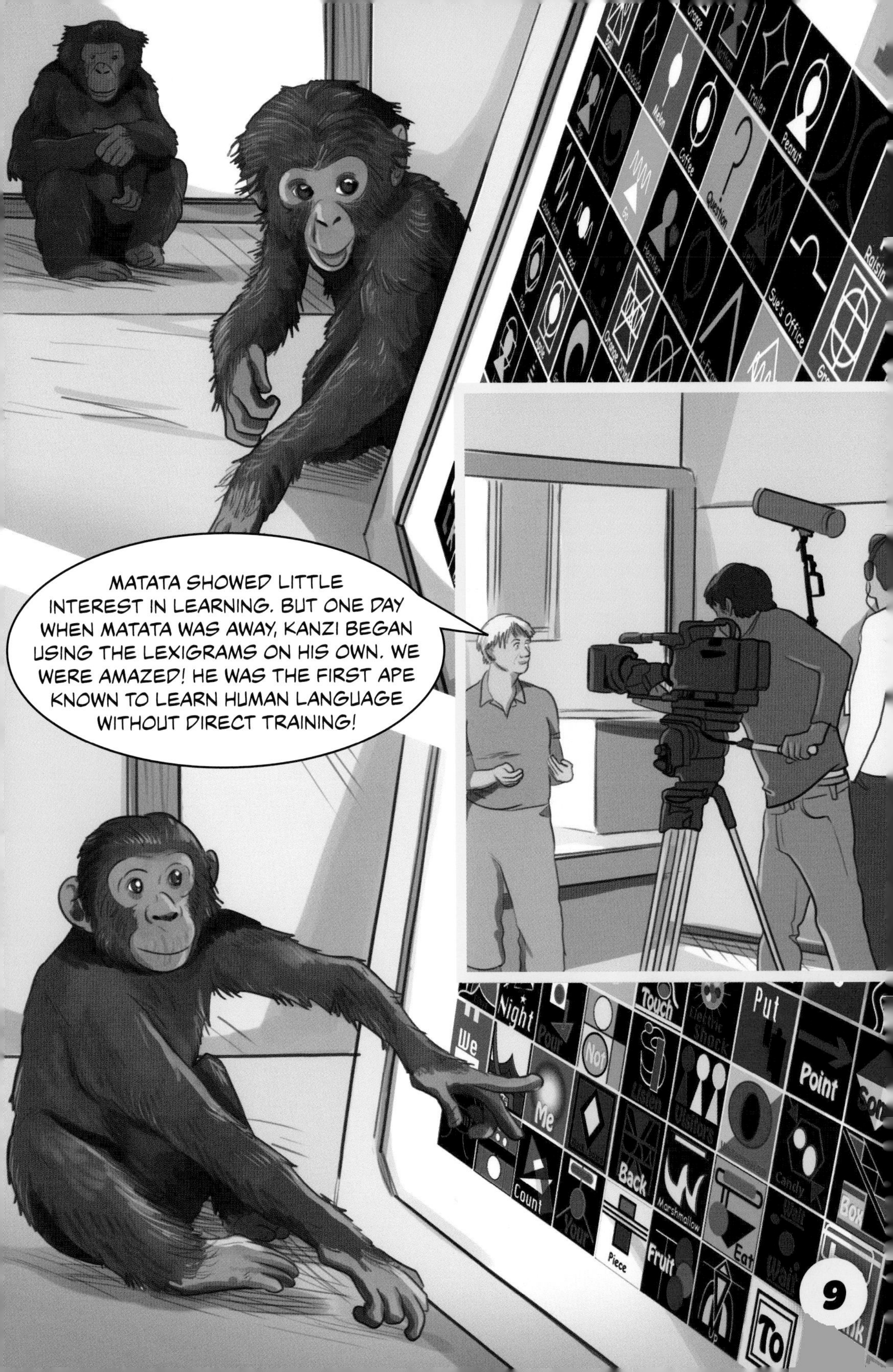
MATATA SHOWED LITTLE INTEREST IN LEARNING. BUT ONE DAY WHEN MATATA WAS AWAY, KANZI BEGAN USING THE LEXIGRAMS ON HIS OWN. WE WERE AMAZED! HE WAS THE FIRST APE KNOWN TO LEARN HUMAN LANGUAGE WITHOUT DIRECT TRAINING!

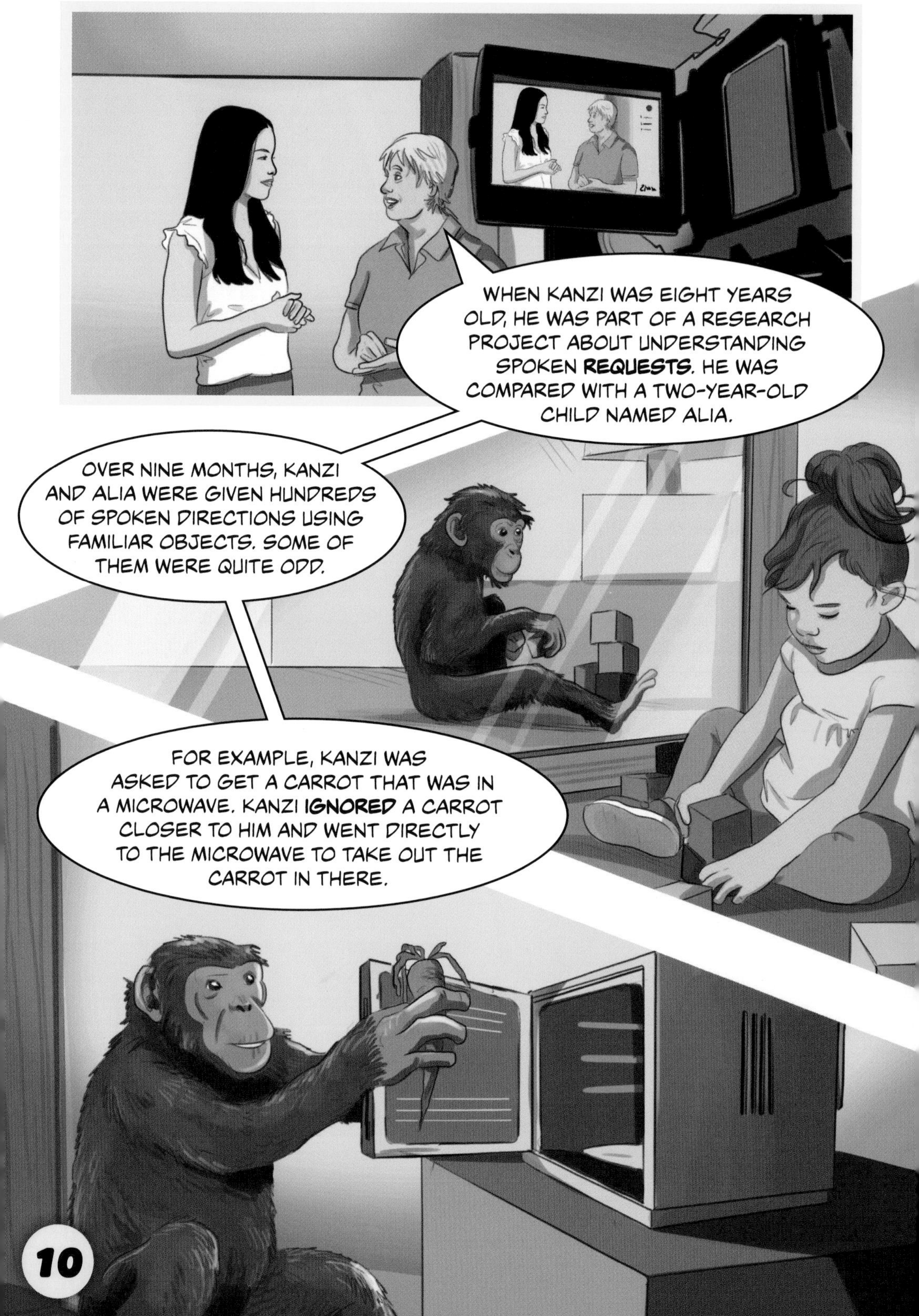
WHEN KANZI WAS EIGHT YEARS OLD, HE WAS PART OF A RESEARCH PROJECT ABOUT UNDERSTANDING SPOKEN **REQUESTS**. HE WAS COMPARED WITH A TWO-YEAR-OLD CHILD NAMED ALIA.
OVER NINE MONTHS, KANZI AND ALIA WERE GIVEN HUNDREDS OF SPOKEN DIRECTIONS USING FAMILIAR OBJECTS. SOME OF THEM WERE QUITE ODD.
FOR EXAMPLE, KANZI WAS ASKED TO GET A CARROT THAT WAS IN A MICROWAVE. KANZI **IGNORED** A CARROT CLOSER TO HIM AND WENT DIRECTLY TO THE MICROWAVE TO TAKE OUT THE CARROT IN THERE.

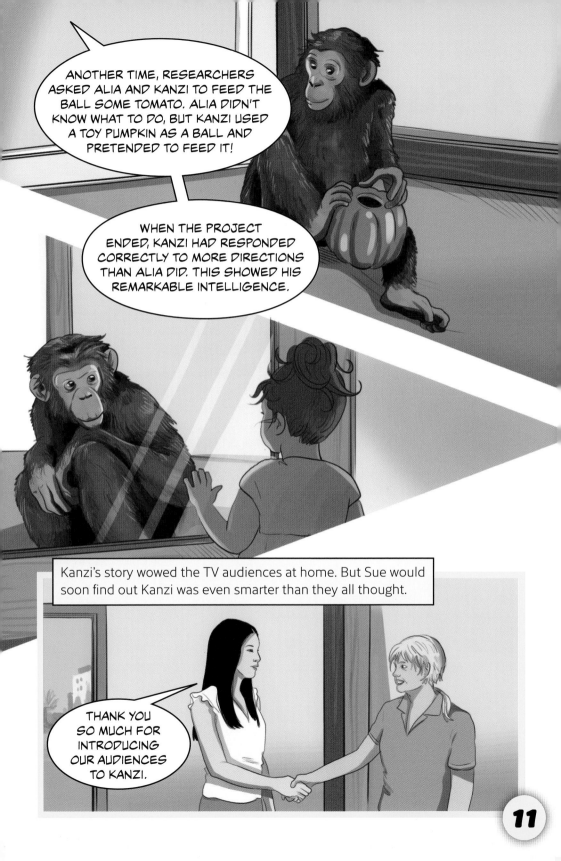

ANOTHER TIME, RESEARCHERS ASKED ALIA AND KANZI TO FEED THE BALL SOME TOMATO. ALIA DIDN'T KNOW WHAT TO DO, BUT KANZI USED A TOY PUMPKIN AS A BALL AND PRETENDED TO FEED IT!

WHEN THE PROJECT ENDED, KANZI HAD RESPONDED CORRECTLY TO MORE DIRECTIONS THAN ALIA DID. THIS SHOWED HIS REMARKABLE INTELLIGENCE.

Kanzi's story wowed the TV audiences at home. But Sue would soon find out Kanzi was even smarter than they all thought.

THANK YOU SO MUCH FOR INTRODUCING OUR AUDIENCES TO KANZI.

CHAPTER 3

A Surprise for Kanzi

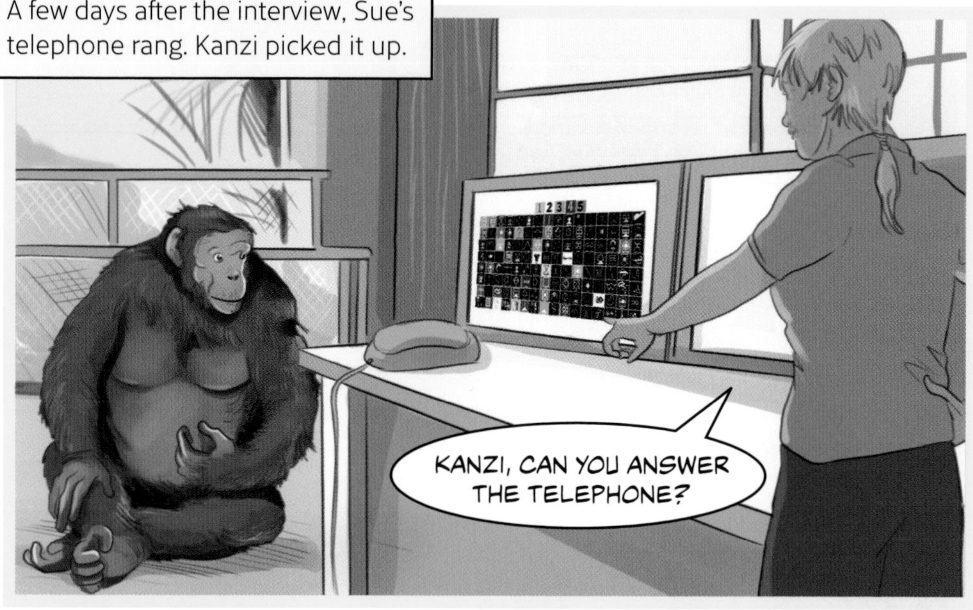
A few days after the interview, Sue's telephone rang. Kanzi picked it up.
KANZI, CAN YOU ANSWER THE TELEPHONE?

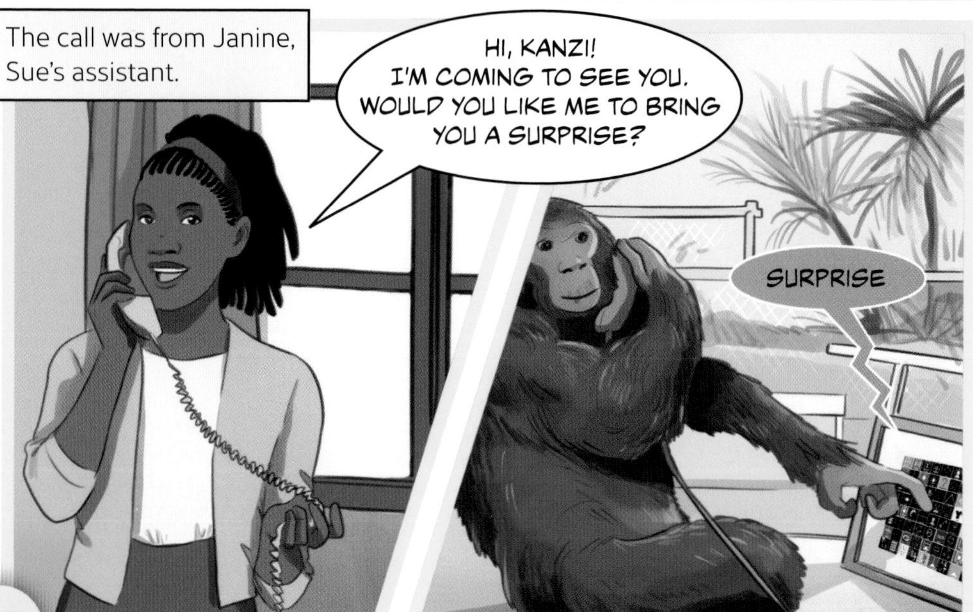
The call was from Janine, Sue's assistant.
HI, KANZI! I'M COMING TO SEE YOU. WOULD YOU LIKE ME TO BRING YOU A SURPRISE?
SURPRISE

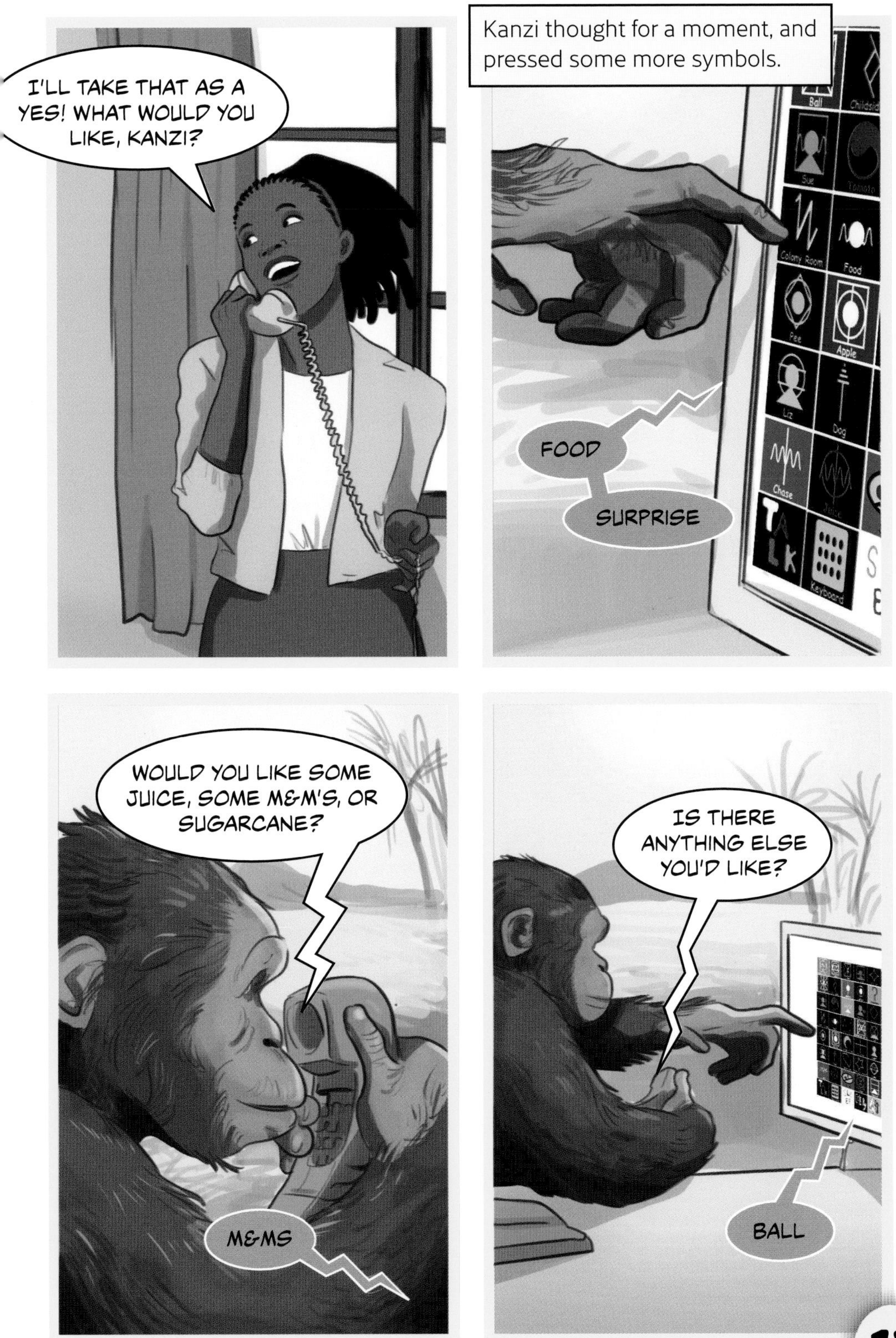
I'LL TAKE THAT AS A YES! WHAT WOULD YOU LIKE, KANZI?
Kanzi thought for a moment, and pressed some more symbols.
Ball
Sue
Tomato
Colony Room
Food
Pee
Apple
Liz
Dog
Chase
TALK
Keyboard
FOOD
SURPRISE
WOULD YOU LIKE SOME JUICE, SOME M&M'S, OR SUGARCANE?
M&MS
IS THERE ANYTHING ELSE YOU'D LIKE?
BALL

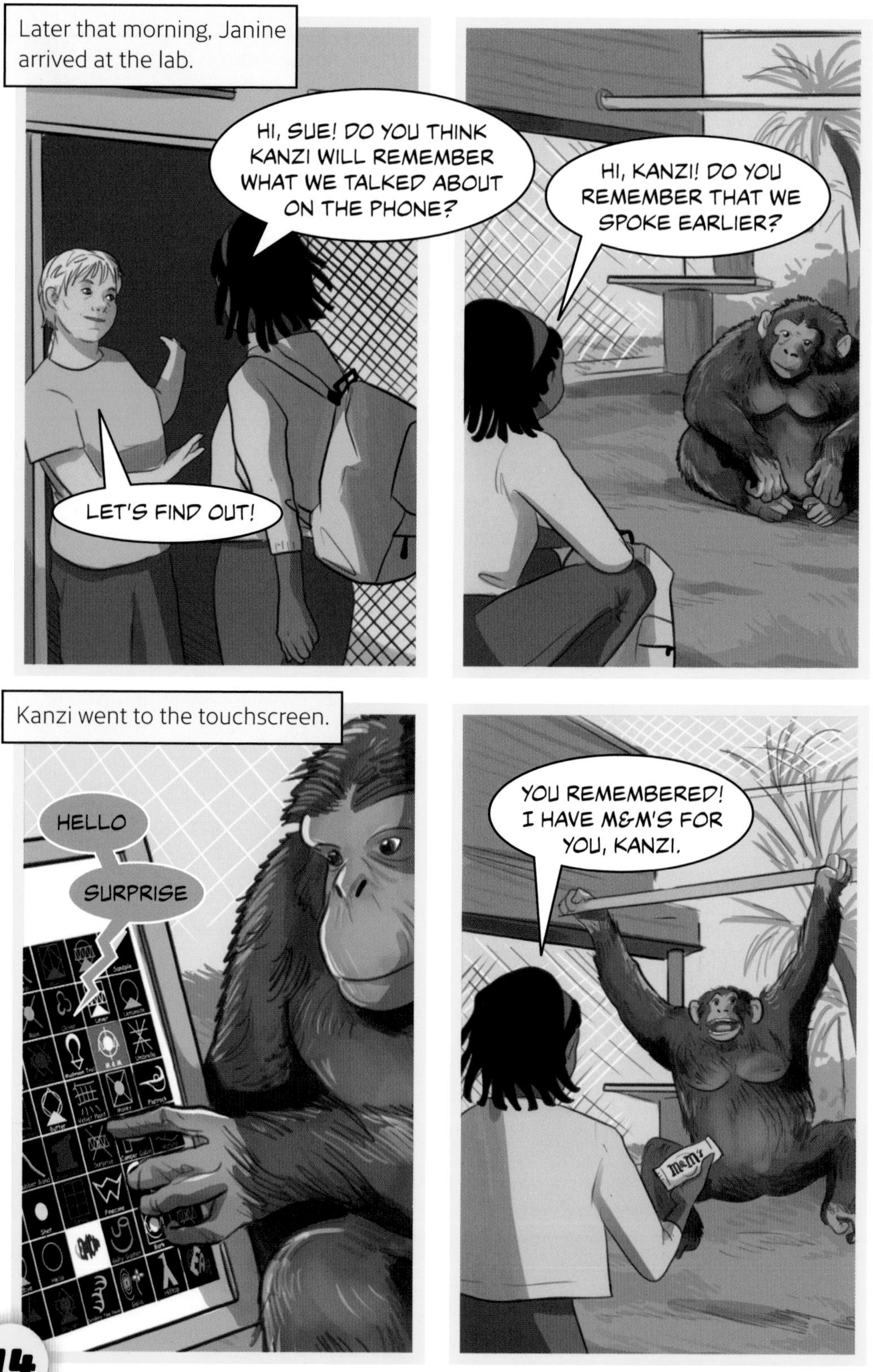
Later that morning, Janine arrived at the lab.
HI, SUE! DO YOU THINK KANZI WILL REMEMBER WHAT WE TALKED ABOUT ON THE PHONE?
LET'S FIND OUT!
HI, KANZI! DO YOU REMEMBER THAT WE SPOKE EARLIER?
Kanzi went to the touchscreen.
HELLO
SURPRISE
YOU REMEMBERED! I HAVE M&M'S FOR YOU, KANZI.

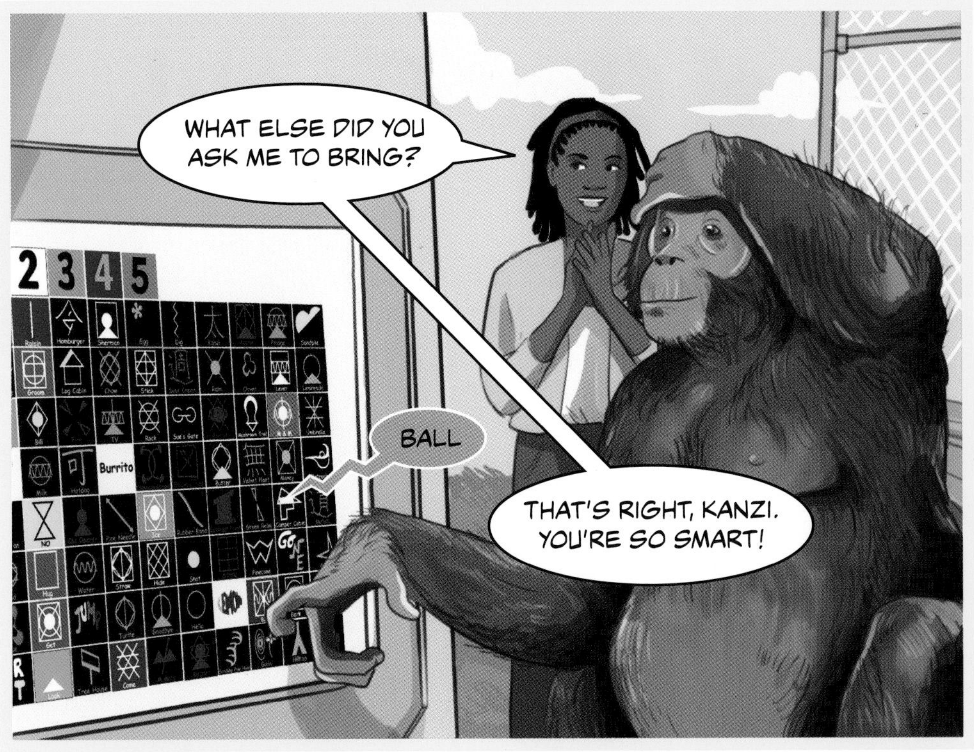
WHAT ELSE DID YOU ASK ME TO BRING?
BALL
THAT'S RIGHT, KANZI. YOU'RE SO SMART!
2 3 4 5
Burrito

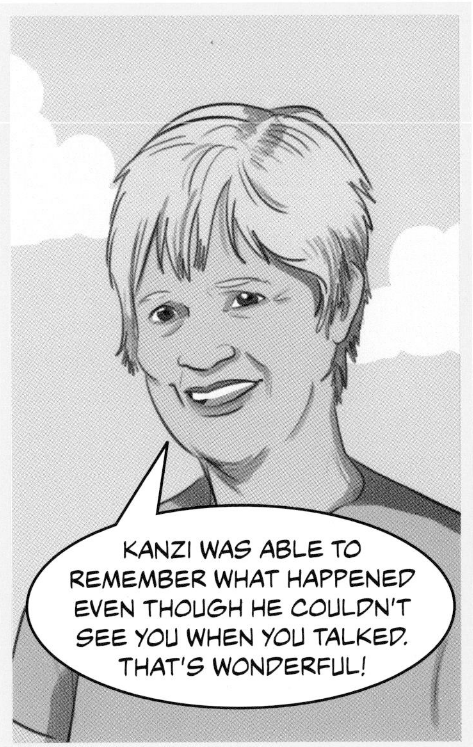
KANZI WAS ABLE TO REMEMBER WHAT HAPPENED EVEN THOUGH HE COULDN'T SEE YOU WHEN YOU TALKED. THAT'S WONDERFUL!

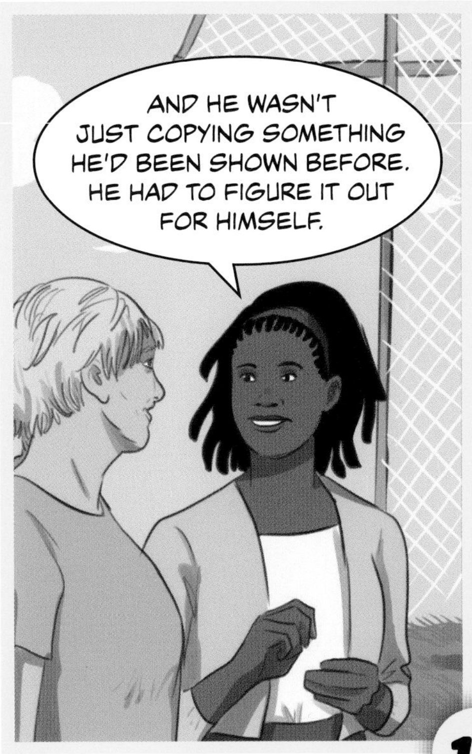
AND HE WASN'T JUST COPYING SOMETHING HE'D BEEN SHOWN BEFORE. HE HAD TO FIGURE IT OUT FOR HIMSELF.

CHAPTER 4

Kanzi Can Cook!

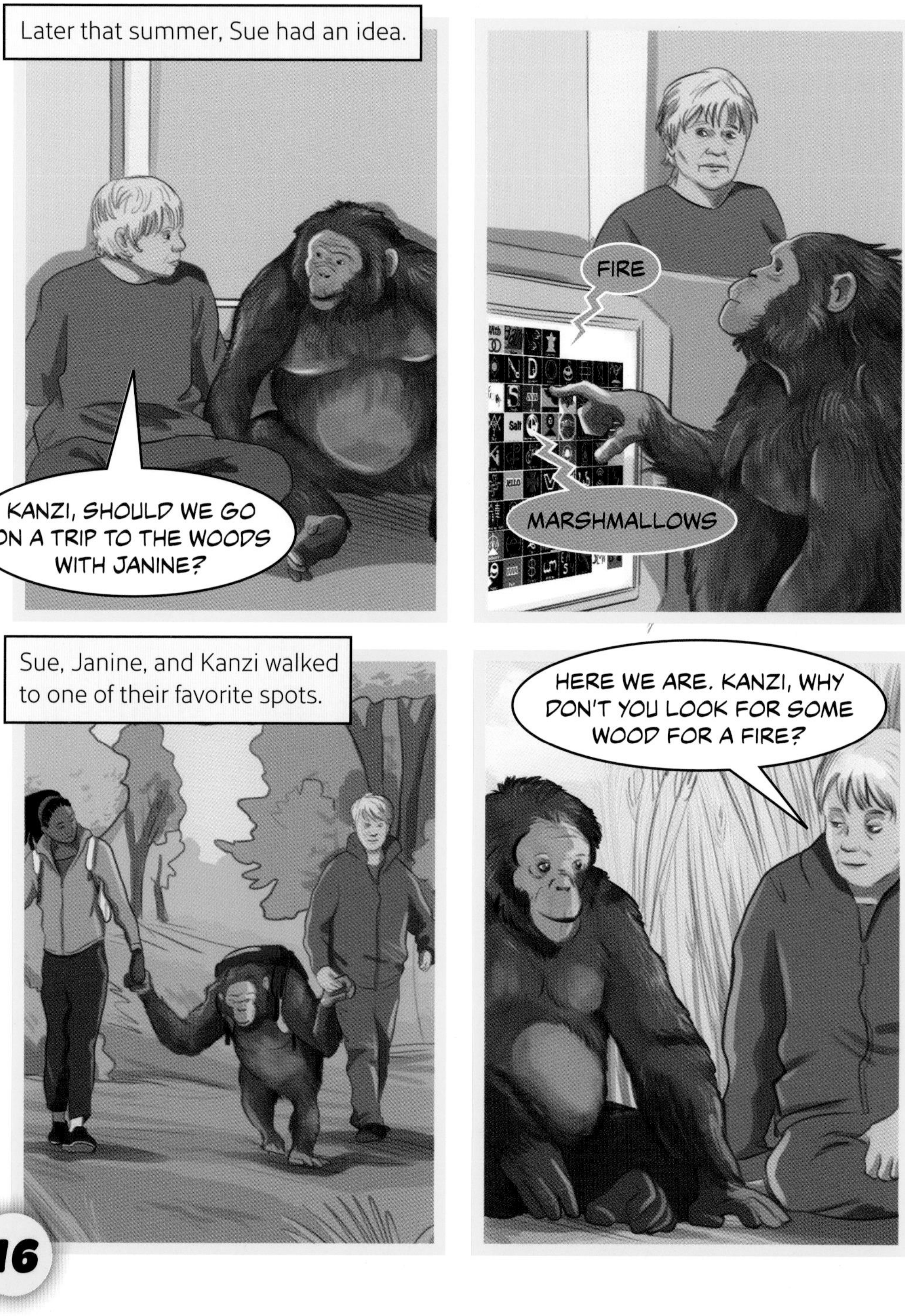
Later that summer, Sue had an idea.
KANZI, SHOULD WE GO ON A TRIP TO THE WOODS WITH JANINE?
FIRE
MARSHMALLOWS
Sue, Janine, and Kanzi walked to one of their favorite spots.
HERE WE ARE. KANZI, WHY DON'T YOU LOOK FOR SOME WOOD FOR A FIRE?

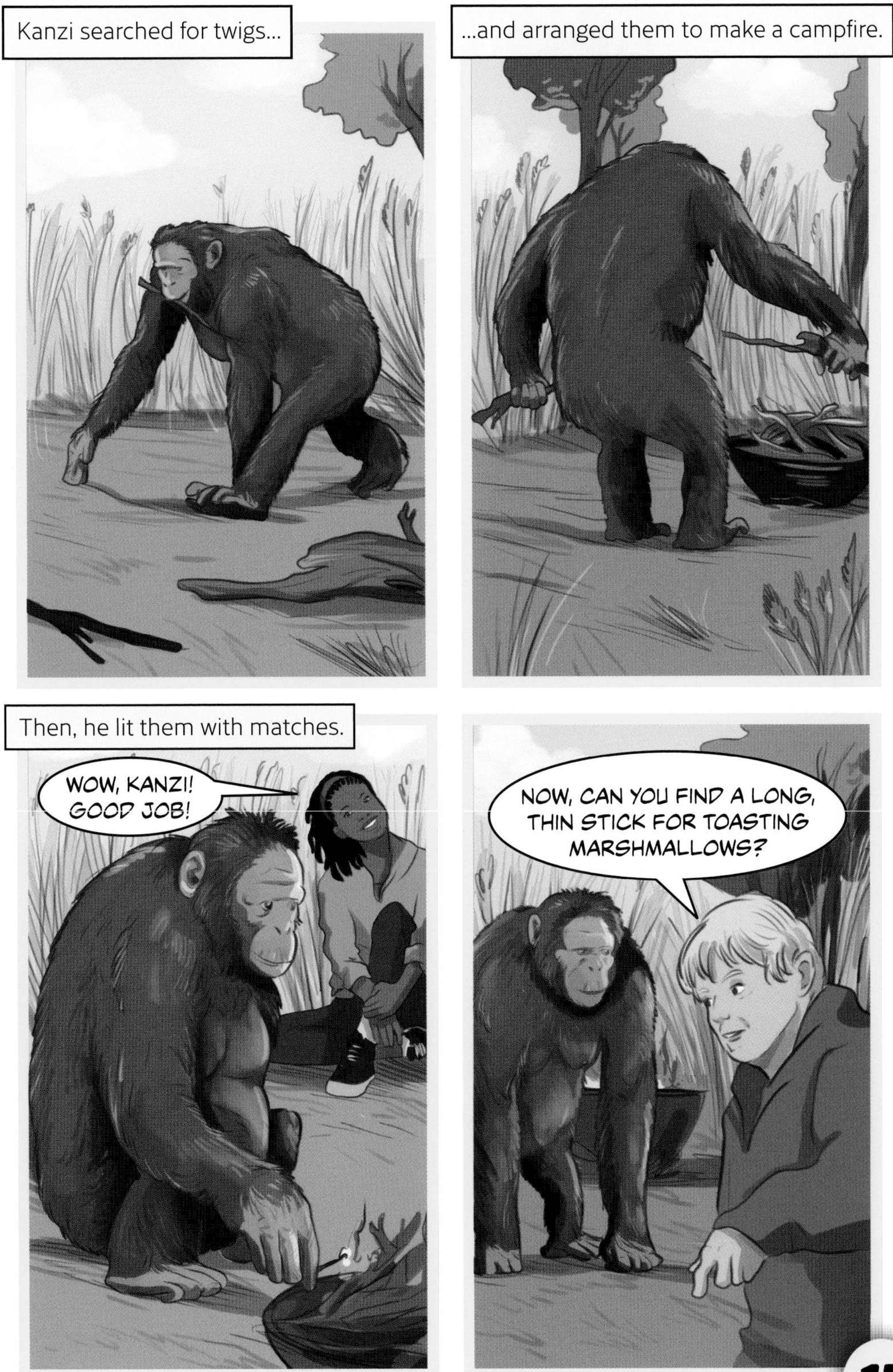
Kanzi searched for twigs...
...and arranged them to make a campfire.
Then, he lit them with matches.
WOW, KANZI! GOOD JOB!
NOW, CAN YOU FIND A LONG, THIN STICK FOR TOASTING MARSHMALLOWS?

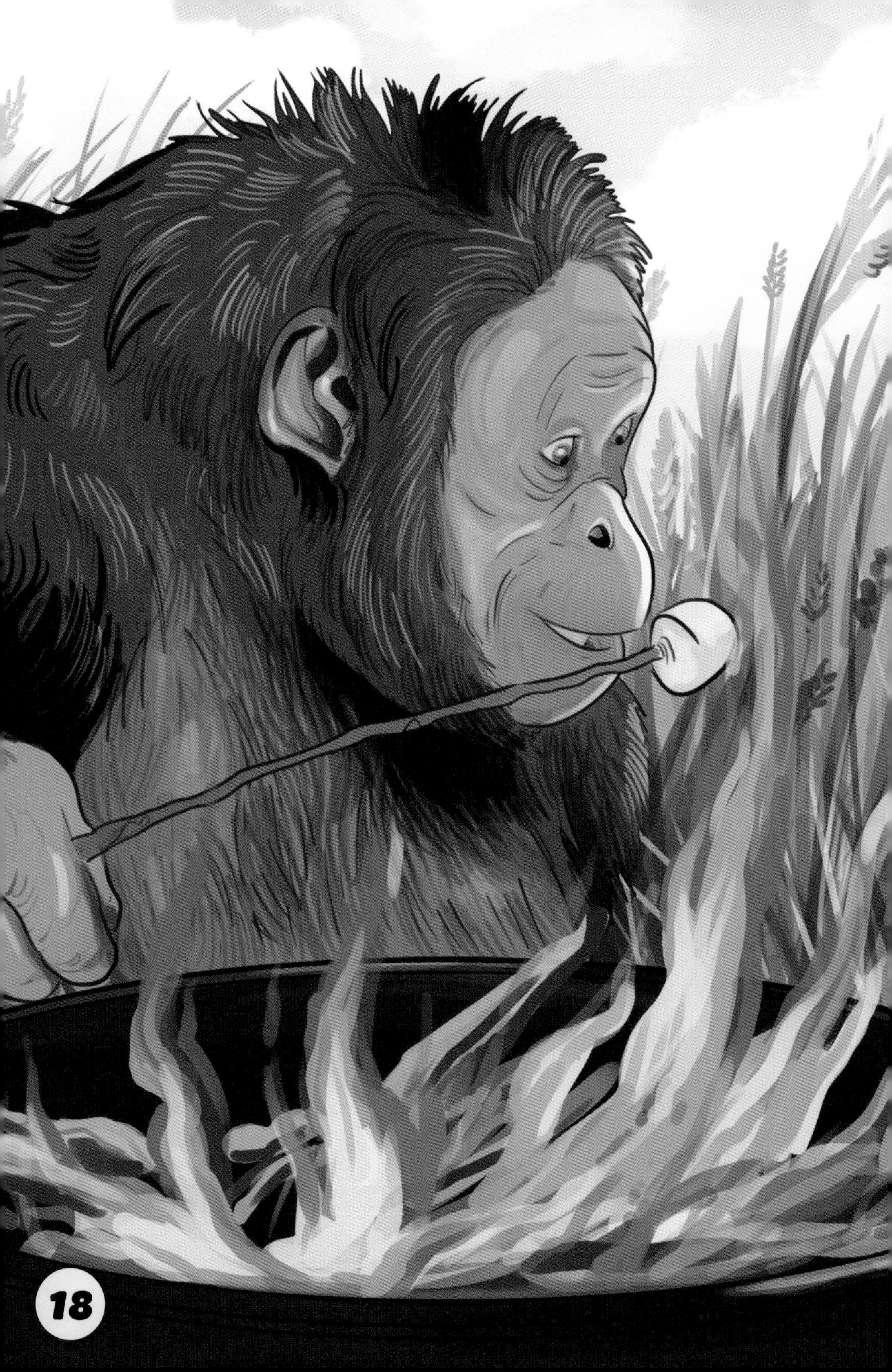

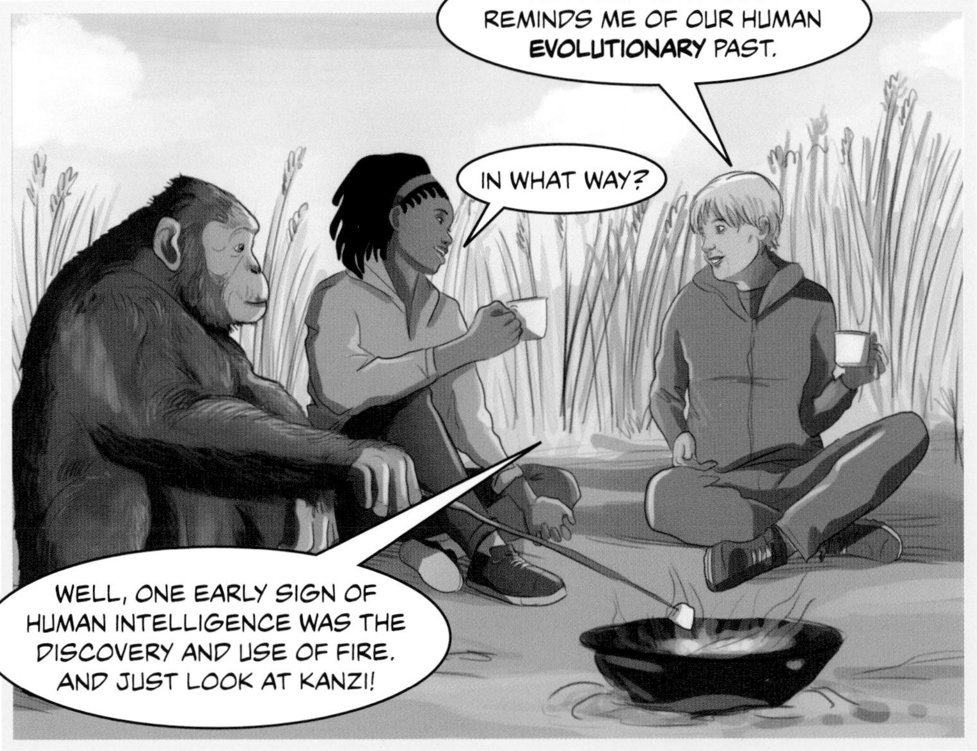
WORKING WITH KANZI REMINDS ME OF OUR HUMAN **EVOLUTIONARY** PAST.
IN WHAT WAY?
WELL, ONE EARLY SIGN OF HUMAN INTELLIGENCE WAS THE DISCOVERY AND USE OF FIRE. AND JUST LOOK AT KANZI!

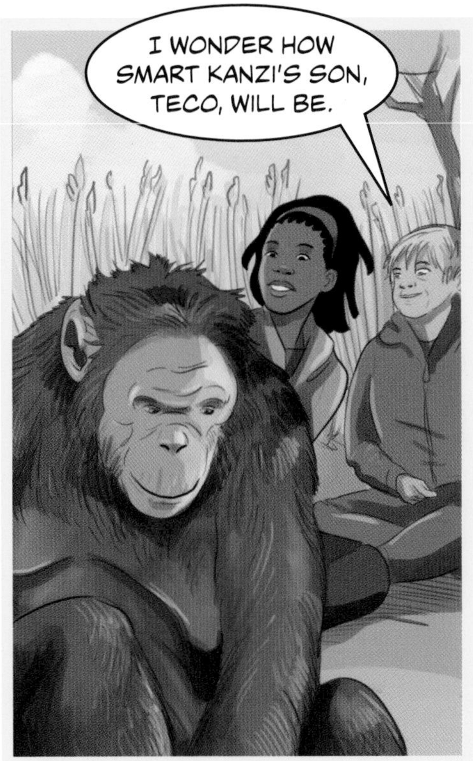
I WONDER HOW SMART KANZI'S SON, TECO, WILL BE.

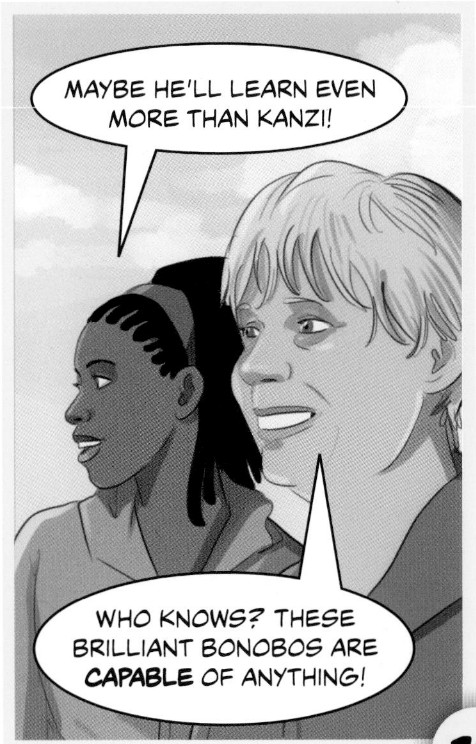
MAYBE HE'LL LEARN EVEN MORE THAN KANZI!
WHO KNOWS? THESE BRILLIANT BONOBOS ARE **CAPABLE** OF ANYTHING!

All about Bonobos

Bonobos are a type of great ape. Other great apes include gorillas, chimpanzees, and orangutans. They were given the name because of their large size and human-like features. Let's learn more facts about the supersmart bonobo!

- Bonobo groups are usually led by an older female that makes important decisions for the whole group.

YOUNG BONOBOS LEARN TO COPY THEIR PARENTS.

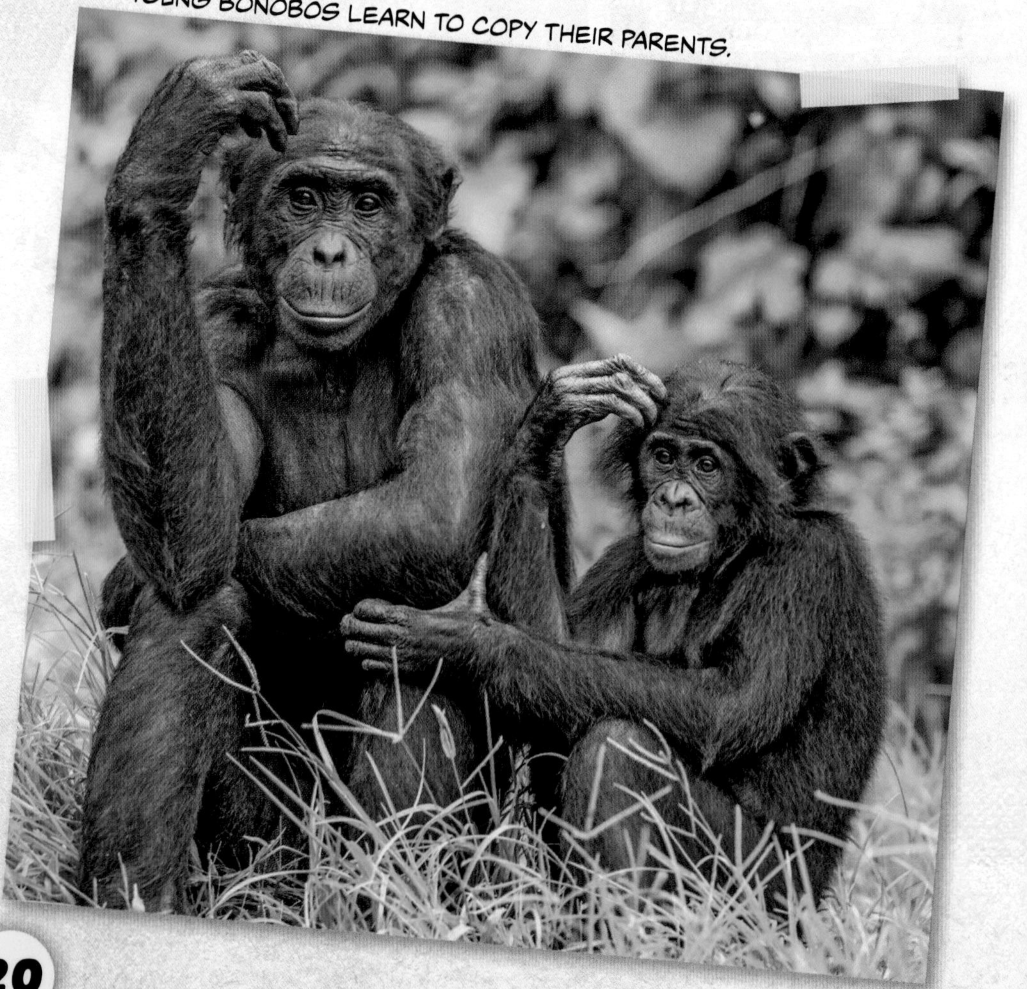

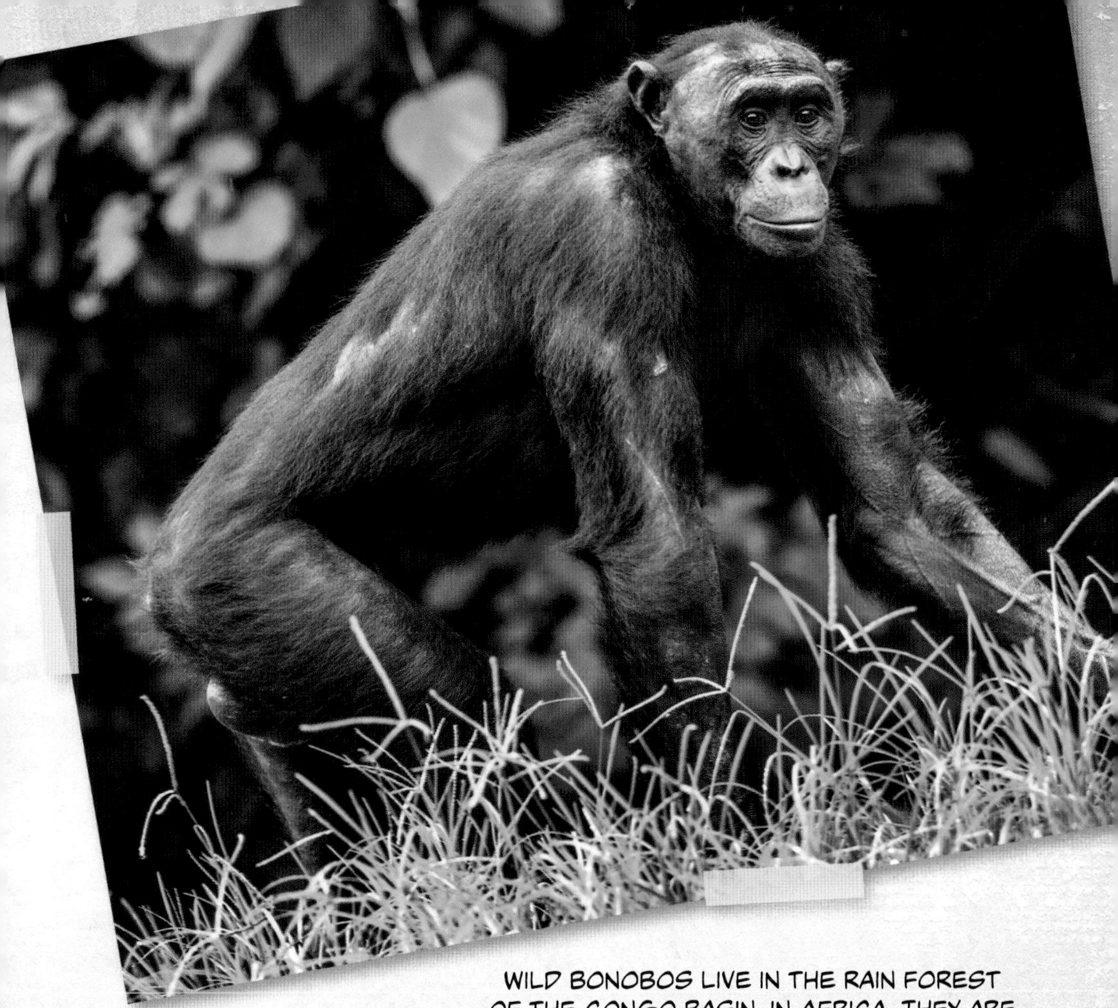

WILD BONOBOS LIVE IN THE RAIN FOREST OF THE CONGO BASIN, IN AFRICA. THEY ARE **ENDANGERED** ANIMALS.

- Bonobos eat mainly leaves, shoots, and fruit. But these animals are **omnivores**. They will eat meat as well as plants.
- Bonobos can weigh up to 85 pounds (40 kg).
- Scientists believe bonobos are one of the closest living relatives to humans. They share behaviors that are similar to ours. Bonobos use tools to get food, and they teach their babies manners.
- They are friendly animals that live peacefully together. Bonobos will work as a team for the good of their group.

More Smart Apes

Scientists studying a group of 106 chimpanzees were amazed by one named Natasha. The scientists tested the chimps by giving them different puzzles to solve. In all of the tests, Natasha had the highest scores. She was able solve the puzzles much faster than her peers. Scientists called Natasha a chimpanzee genius!

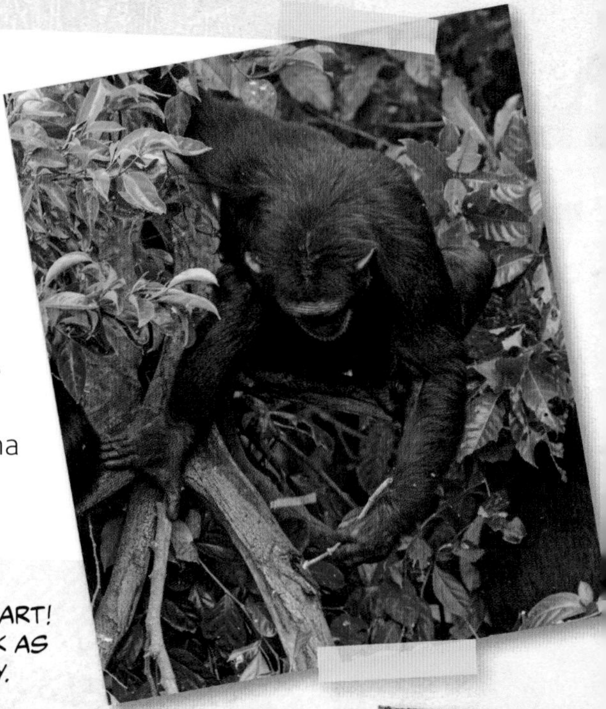

CHIMPANZEES ARE SUPERSMART! THIS CHIMP IS USING A STICK AS A TOOL TO GATHER HONEY.

A gorilla named Koko was taught sign language by Dr. Francine Patterson, a scientist studying animal intelligence. Koko learned to sign more than 1,000 words and used them to **communicate** with Dr. Patterson. She learned the words for many different things including *toy*, *apple*, *dog*, and *cookie*. Koko could sign complicated emotions, such as *sad* and *love*, and she could express when she liked or did not like things.

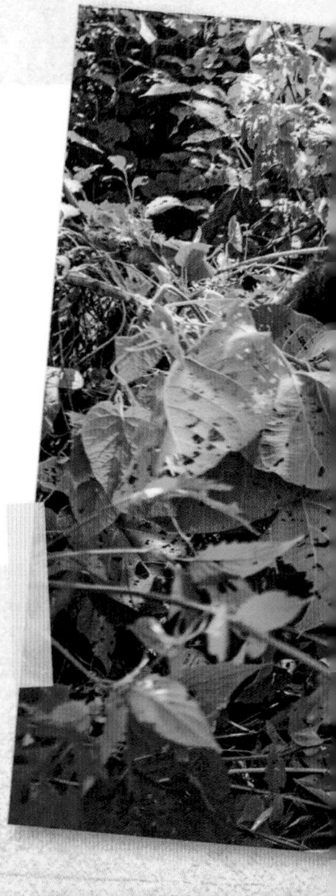

Glossary

capable able to do something

communicate to express ideas or emotions to someone or something else

endangered in danger of dying out

evolutionary the historical development of a group

ignored not noticed or paid attention to

impressive having qualities that are admirable

intelligent able to learn

lexigrams symbols that represent words

omnivores animals that eat both plants and meat

requests things that have been asked for

research to study in order to find our more about something

symbols images that have meanings

IN THE WILD, GORILLAS
COMMUNICATE USING SOUNDS
AND MOVEMENTS.

Index

Read More

Mattern, Joanne. *Chimpanzees (Blastoff Readers: The World's Smartest Animals)*. Minneapolis: Bellwether Media, 2021.

Mattern, Joanne. *Smartest Animals (Earth's Amazing Animals: Animal Top 10)*. Egremont, MA: Red Chair Press, 2020.

Murray, Julie. *Gorillas (Animal Kingdom)*. Minneapolis: ABDO Publishing, 2020.

Learn More Online

1. Go to **www.factsurfer.com** or scan the QR code below.
2. Enter "**Kanzi Learns Language**" into the search box.
3. Click on the cover of this book to see a list of websites.